THE BREAKTHROUGH POWER OF MEDITATION

YOUR SUPERNATURAL SOURCE OF UNLIMITED INCREASE

The Teaching Ministry of Dr. E.L. Womack, Sr.

©2015 Womack House Publishing, LLC

Published in the United States of America

Womack House Publishing, LLC
3965 East Brookstown Drive
Baton Rouge, LA 70805
info@womackhouse.com
(225) 357-1330

ISBN 978-0-9904219-1-7 (pbk)

LCN 2015919812

**For information about special discounts for bulk purchases
contact Womack House Publishing, LLC.**

CONTENTS

Dedication. 5

Introduction 6

Chapter 1: What Is Meditation?. 11
Personal Meditation Exercise and Activity. 20

Chapter 2: Meditate Day & Night 22

Chapter 3: Using Your Imagination to Meditate. . . . 32

Chapter 4: Change Your Image of Yourself. 38
The "I Am" Exercise 48

Chapter 5: The Power of the Tongue 50
The "Speak Life" Exercise 55

Chapter 6: We Are More Than Able 56

Chapter 7: Beware of Your Environment 64

Chapter 8: Renew Your Mind 71

Conclusion 82

Prayer for Salvation 85

DEDICATION

Thanks to God, who gives us the victory through our Lord Jesus Christ. To Audrey, my partner in life and in ministry, I am the world's most blessed man. You have helped shape me into more than I could ever imagine.

My major role was to work and provide for the family; however, your supportive role in my life has been priceless. You have been that virtuous woman always building and challenging me.

To my children, Ada, Alison, Ingrid, Myra, Bryan, and Emmerine Jr., your love and support drive my life. I love you for who you are and all that you will accomplish in life. Also in loving memory of my oldest son, Bernard, and to all of my colleagues and friends that support me.

Dr. E. L. Womack, Sr.

INTRODUCTION

You know it's time. You know there's more. You just can't figure out what it is that you're missing. More often within the Kingdom of God, Christians are wondering, what's going on with the transfer? Where is my double portion? Where is my 100-fold return? Well, the time has come for you to tap into another level for success. It's time for your advancement. In the body of Christ, many people are not advancing, because they are not meditating in the Word of God. They don't understand meditation according to biblical principles. Meditation goes along with vision. Many today have a lot of Word in them, but they don't know how to use meditation to get the job done. Meditation means filling your thoughts with the thoughts of God and being consumed with the things God has said. When you consume yourself with what God has said, you will see what he said and then do what he says. Everything we meditate on must come from God's Word. Many are consumed with the things of the world, debt, bills, problems, and circumstances so they can't give God any time. They don't have time to meditate on the Word of God or come to church and play an active part in the things of God.

God deals with our thought life using principles and spiritual laws. **He knew that when we came into the family of God our spirit man would be changed but we would have to do something with our minds.** This is why he tells us to meditate day and night to renew our minds in the Word of God. God enlightens us by sharing with us that His thoughts are not our thoughts. He does not think like the world system thinks. We are thinking in line with what the world system has said about us and try to do everything according to that rather than according to what God has said.

Before I married, I prayed to God for a wife after Vietnam. I described to God exactly what I wanted and had envisioned in my mind. I asked God for her that weekend when I prayed. When I saw her that weekend, I could have married her that day. What I imagined in prayer I received in a couple of days and later in marriage. Forty-five years later, with seven kids, I am still married to the love of my life.

The thought life is very important to us. We must learn to become saturated with God's Word and begin to see what God sees in the Word. Therefore our thoughts must come from the Word of God. The images that we should be receiving should come from the Word of God instead of from TV or things we see in the natural realm. We try to take the thoughts of the world and bring them into the church and into our lives to make God line up with those thoughts, but it won't work. This causes us to limit ourselves and prevents us from getting a breakthrough and going to the level that God wants to take us. God is constantly telling us his thoughts and ways are higher. We must learn to put our thoughts aside, to take up the nature of God, and to begin to think in line with the Word of God. **If you can't see what God sees, how then will you obtain it?**

The lack of understanding concerning meditation is holding a lot of people back. Many are not prospering in life, because they don't have a vision, they are not meditating on the Word of God, and they do not know what meditation is. Some religions believe that meditating is trying to keep your mind blank, but that's not meditating. You must fill your thoughts with the Word of God and allow the Word of God to begin to build images in your life. You must be able to see what God says in His Word.

> **Practicing meditation gives vision, insight, and in-depth conception.**

I have more understanding than all my teachers:
for thy testimonies are my meditation.
PSALM 119:99

The writer says he has more understanding and a deeper insight than all of his teachers because of his testimonies or meditation. Testimony means witness or words. This means his thought life is not the same as regular people; it is consumed and lines up with the Word of God, which is his testimony. He has insight into the plan and things of God for his life. Through meditating on the Word of God, his life has changed. Meditation brings clarity and understanding to your heart. You must be saturated with the thoughts of God, words of God, and things of God and allow them to build an image in your life.

When I came into the family of God, I did not know anything about success in life. I thought you must merely get a job and work hard to take care of your responsibility and family (wife, kids, and bills). But when I became born again, the Lord gave me a vision and said to eat the Word of God. He led me to Ezekiel 3:2–3:

So I opened my mouth, and he caused me to eat the roll.
And he said unto me, Son of man, cause thy belly to eat,
and fill thy bowels with this roll that I give thee.
Then did I eat it; and it was in my mouth
as honey for sweetness.

I did not understand it. So I started to write the promises down on 4x4 cards and began to speak them out loud while on my job, placing them on the wall while laying bricks. I would speak God's promises and absorb the Word, which is a type of meditation that changed my life. Meditating on God's Word will change your life and raise you up to a higher level of life you desire. The body of Christ must start meditating on God's Word.

Throughout this book I will enlighten you to change your thoughts, ideas, and concepts as you speak the promises of God's Word aloud.

For my thoughts are not your thoughts,
neither are your ways my ways, saith the LORD.
For as the heavens are higher than the earth,
so are my ways higher than your ways,
and my thoughts than your thoughts.
For as the rain cometh down, and the snow from heaven,
and returneth not thither, but watereth the earth,
and maketh it bring forth and bud,
that it may give seed to the sower, and bread to the eater:
So shall my word be that goeth forth out of my mouth:
it shall not return unto me void,
but it shall accomplish that which I please,
and it shall prosper in the thing whereto I sent it.

ISAIAH 55:8–11

The purpose of this teaching is to get God's people to meditate on the Word of God, to allow the law of visualization to be manifest in their lives, and to get God's people to see spiritually.

If you are expecting God to do something great in your life, your thinking must change first! When your thinking changes, your situation will change because you have changed!

Chapter 1:
What Is Meditation?

"The Power Is in the Gospel"

According to *Strong's Concordance*, the word meditate means to mutter, to ponder, to speak, to study, to talk, to utter, to gaze, to murmur, and to imagine. If you are expecting to do anything for God, to change your life, or to go to another level, you must learn how to meditate on the Word of God. If we learn how to meditate on the Word of God in every situation that arises in our lives, we will get the victory and make our way successful and prosperous.

Have you ever been in a situation where you were going to take a test, but you didn't spend as much time studying as you should have? At the last minute, you start reviewing your notes faster and faster to get the information in you. You begin to ponder the word. This is a type of meditation. In studying, I was made aware of the following:

1. People that hear the word will retain 10–20% of what they hear.

2. People that read the word will retain 20–40% of what they read.

3. People that study the word will retain 40–60% of what they study.

4. People that memorize the word will retain 60–80% of what they memorize.

5. People that meditate on the word will retain 80–100% of what they meditate upon.

You need to take God's Word, speak it over and over, and use your imagination to see the end result of what God is saying to you on a daily basis. This is not wishful thinking; the Word of God is the substance. Let's began to use our imaginations for their best use, which is in line with God's Word. You should close your eyes, speak God's word, and use your imagination (mind) to see it coming to fruition in your life.

This is one area where the body of Christ is not entering into because of too many distractions. Throughout the body of Christ, many people are in the same situation they were in many years ago because they are not using their imagination and meditation properly. Once they do, they will be able to change the wrong things that are housed in their subconscious mind. It will not happen overnight, but you must start somewhere. The best place to begin is by meditating on the Word of God day and night.

*This book of the law shall not depart out of thy mouth;
but thou shalt meditate therein day and night,
that thou mayest observe to do according to all that
is written therein: for then thou shalt make thy way
prosperous, and then thou shalt have good success.*

JOSHUA 1:8

In order to make quality decisions and go forth making your way prosperous, line your words and subconscious up accordingly with the Word of God. God desires the best for you, and he wants you to rise up to another level in life. He would not have given us the promises and principles if he didn't want them to manifest in our lives.

*I will meditate also of all thy work,
and talk of thy doings.*

PSALM 77:12

He is saying I will meditate and talk about what God is doing. I will think about and say the things God has said in His Word. I will proclaim it night and day. You need to change your surroundings. You may be in poverty now, but begin to speak, meditate upon, and gaze at the Word day and night, and your image and outlook will change. The things around you will begin to change supernaturally. Put the Word of God in your mouth, talk about it, and get it in your heart.

*Give ear to my words, O LORD,
consider my meditation.*

PSALM 5:1

13

David is saying, Lord, consider my thoughts, my talking about your word, my gazing at your word, my murmuring of your word.

> *But the Comforter, which is the Holy Ghost,*
> *whom the Father will send in my name,*
> *he shall teach you all things, and bring all things*
> *to your remembrance, whatsoever I have said unto you.*
>
> JOHN 14:26

God wants you to store the Word in your heart so that the Holy Spirit can bring it to your remembrance. This is the Holy Spirit's job, but if you have not meditated on anything, he does not have anything to bring to your remembrance. If you do not know what the Lord has said, or not meditating day and night, or not taking the word of God and gazing at it, and are not using your imagination to see what God has said in His Word, how can the Holy Spirit bring something to your remembrance? He cannot do it! Change comes when you change your way of thinking in line with what the Word of God says. Remember, God's way of thinking is higher than our way of thinking. You must get the thoughts of God in you through His Word and allow those thoughts to consume your mind; then you will be able to make quality decisions in life. Joshua made quality decisions and was prosperous in all areas of his life because he meditated day and night.

PUT YOUR IMAGINATION TO WORK

Sometimes we think it's hard or that we don't have time, but I challenge you to make it a priority in your life. Take a scripture of what you are believing God for, read the scripture, close your eyes, and begin to see that scripture coming alive. Begin to use your imagination to see doors opening for you. Do this for five minutes in the morning and five minutes at night every day. Talk about it, and keep it before you. Supernaturally, the word of God will change the image you have, and you will begin to see yourself differently. We must learn to see ourselves the way God sees us regardless of how it looks in the natural, because we operate according to God's principles.

All of us have been to a doctor at one point in our life, whether the appointment was positive or negative. Isaiah 53:4–5 states:

Surely he hath borne our griefs, and carried our sorrows:
yet we did esteem him stricken, smitten of God, and afflicted.
But he was wounded for our transgressions, he was
bruised for our iniquities:
the chastisement of our peace was upon him;
and with his stripes we are healed.

ISAIAH 53:4–5

The most important thing God is trying to show us is to use our imagination (mind) to see what God sees in His Word. You must be able to see what God says in His Word in order to get the victory you have been looking for. Through meditating, the creative ability of God is developed on the inside of your heart. When the Word is developed on the inside of your heart, you will be able to see, to paint pictures, and to use your imagination. However, many within the body of Christ are seeing the wrong thing, imagining the wrong thing, and painting the wrong image of their lives. They are seeing themselves as a failure and not as a winner—meditating upon their debts, problems, doctor's report, and circumstances and talking about their failures. When saying what can't be done, situations are dim and not victorious. This is not what our heavenly Father intended.

> *The entrance of thy words giveth light;*
> *it giveth understanding unto the simple.*
> PSALM 119:130

You cannot meditate on something you do not have inside you.

The Word of God must first be in your mouth to get into your heart. What you meditate upon is what you will see on a daily basis—I dealt with this in depth in my book entitled *The Seed Is in God's Word.* The things God wants to do for you must be conceived in your spirit before they can become a reality in your life. You must get it in you first before you can get images and paint pictures of the Word. What you see is what you will attract into your life. Meditating is also a form of talking. What you talk about all the time is what you will see. It works both ways—if you meditate, ponder, or speak on the wrong thing, you will have images of the wrong thing in your mind. Another word for meditating is gazing. If you gaze at defeat, problems, and circumstances, that is what you will attract in your life.

Meditate upon these things; give thyself wholly to them;
that thy profiting may appear to all.
Take heed unto thyself, and unto the doctrine;
continue in them: for in doing this
thou shalt both save thyself, and them that hear thee.
1 TIMOTHY 4:15-16

Paul told Timothy to meditate on the Word, speak the Word, talk about the Word, gaze at the Word, and paint an image of the Word; use your imagination to see what the Word is saying, and you will profit from it. The word profit means to advance, to progress in life, to increase, to grow, and to benefit. **God wants you to profit from the Word and from meditating.** Take it seriously. God is a God who wants His people to profit and to be successful in life.

BENEFITTING FROM MEDITATING

As you meditate in the Word, and apply it into your life on a daily basis. These are a few of the benefits:

1. Let the Word of God take preeminence in your life, and you surely will profit from the Word of God.

2. The Word of God will cause you to see and bring revelation to your mind and heart.

3. The Word will give increase in your life.

4. You will become more productive in your life as you meditate on the Word of God.

5. You will get excited and go forth in the things of God.

My heart was hot within me,
while I was musing the fire burned:
then spake I with my tongue.

PSALM 39:3

The word musing means meditating. While I was speaking God's Word, talking about God's Word, and gazing at God's Word on a daily basis, the Word began to rise up as a burning in my heart. Meditating on the Word of God is a force that will begin to burn in your heart. It is also being planted into your subconscious mind. The Word will then come forth at the right time, and you will be able to make quality decisions. When the Word begins to burn, you will be able to speak it out. Why do we continue to make carnal decisions? The Word is not burning on the inside. The way to victory and success in life is by meditating on God's Word and painting a picture of what God has said. Many times we do not get to the point where the Word burns on the inside.

You can affect people around you through your mediation in the Word and by applying that Word in your life. The Word will change your image and outlook upon life itself. You are going to have to learn how to use your imagination for righteousness as a form of meditation. Joshua had to do it. Moses had to do it. Abraham had to do it. All the men who were used mightily of

God had to be able to see and understand what God was saying in His Word. Therefore, they had to meditate in the Word day and night so that they could deal wisely in the affairs of life and make quality decisions.

For I know the thoughts that I think toward you,
saith the LORD, thoughts of peace, and not of evil,
to give you an expected end.
JEREMIAH 29:11

Your decision making will never change unless you learn how to meditate in God's Word!

PERSONAL MEDITATION
EXERCISE AND ACTIVITY

This exercise is just a simple guide to assist you in practicing your meditation daily. Meditating, saying and writing the things you desire, and the Word of God will work on your behalf.

So what would you like to see happen in different areas of your life?

Personally I would like to see

_____

_____

Supportive Scripture

_____

Professionally I would like to see

_____

_____

Supportive Scripture

_____

Spiritually I would like to see

_____

_____

Supportive Scripture

_____

Emotionally I would like to see

_____

_____

Supportive Scripture

_____

Intellectually I would like to see

_____

_____

Supportive Scripture

_____

CHAPTER 2:
MEDITATE DAY & NIGHT

This book of the law shall not depart out of thy mouth;
but thou shalt meditate therein day and night, that thou
mayest observe to do according to all that is written
therein: for then thou shalt make thy way prosperous,
and then thou shalt have good success.

JOSHUA 1:8

In order to go to the level where God wants you to go, you must learn how to meditate on the Word of God on a daily basis. In the first chapter of Joshua, God taught Joshua systematically how to meditate on the Word of God, get victory in his life, and go to the next level. God told Joshua that if he would meditate on the Word, he would make Joshua's way prosperous; he would have good success and deal wisely in the affairs of life. Joshua had to meditate on the Word of God and learn how to use his imagination to see what God was saying to him and about him. If Joshua did not understand meditating, he would have been unable to accomplish the things he did for God.

God told Joshua to keep the Word before him by keeping it in his mouth. He had to mutter, ponder, and speak the Word. Joshua had to prosper in three areas: spiritually, mentally (soulish realm), and physically. He used the first five books of the Bible and applied them to his life, and God shared powerful truths with Joshua.

Joshua used three techniques to get the Word in himself:

1. Verbalization – He had to speak, mutter, ponder, and study the Word.

2. Visualization – He had to use his imagination, gaze at the Word, see what God had said on a daily basis, and apply it into his life.

3. Internalization – He had to have the Word working inside of him. The Word was in his heart and in his mind, which resulted in corresponding action.

> *There shall not any man be able to stand*
> *before thee all the days of thy life:*
> *as I was with Moses, so I will be with thee:*
> *I will not fail thee, nor forsake thee.*
> JOSHUA 1:5

God was telling Joshua he must be able to see in order to have the spiritual success and the life that God wanted him to have. God told him that nobody would ever be able to stand in his shoes. God was saying, Joshua, if you keep the Word before you, if you meditate on it day and night, and if you use your imagination day and night to see what I have said in my Word and to let that word paint an image in your life, it will supernaturally come to pass. If you learn this principle, nothing will be able to hold you back.

Now Jericho was straitly shut up because of the children
of Israel: none went out, and none came in.
And the LORD said unto Joshua,
See, I have given into thine hand Jericho,
and the king thereof, and the mighty men of valor.
JOSHUA 6:1–2

God told Joshua he had given him Jericho under one condition—he had to see it. God told Joshua to see. Joshua had two eyes to see with, but God was not talking about his natural eyes. God wanted Joshua to paint an image, to see, to envision. He was talking about his imagination. He wanted him to see within what God had said in His Word. He had to visualize the walls of Jericho on the ground. After Joshua was able to see and observe, he was tested. God gave him specific instructions, but if he was unable to see it, the walls of Jericho would be up today unless God used another method. God spoke to Joshua and gave him the plan, and he went forth and accomplished it through meditation.

You cannot observe to do until you start meditating and seeing it. You must see it within and meditate on it day and night until it begins to saturate you. Then you will see it manifest in your life.

You will be able to walk into the greater blessings of God when you meditate on the Word of God. The Word of God must be in your mouth, and once it gets in your mouth, it gets in your heart.

> *But his delight is in the law of the LORD;*
> *and in his law doth he meditate day and night.*
> *And he shall be like a tree planted by the rivers of water,*
> *that bringeth forth his fruit in his season;*
> *his leaf also shall not wither;*
> *and whatsoever he doeth shall prosper.*
>
> PSALM 1:2–3

Pondering the Word of God helps your belief system. It helps you to believe God and will keep your momentum up, but it must be done consistently. The results of meditation are in verse three: You will bring forth fruit, and whatsoever you do will prosper. Do not meditate just to get something or only until you get what you want—it must become a lifestyle. Evaluate what you are doing on a daily basis. Meditating on the Word of God will change your image and outlook upon life. A tree that is planted by the rivers of water receives all the nourishment it needs. It is constantly getting fresh water and growing. We can grow and be blessed like the tree. You can bring forth your fruit in your season. God wants to bless you, but He will not violate His principles to bless you. You must line up with His Word. God intends for us to use meditation to take us to higher heights. Day and night in verse two means that it is a continuous process. It should be done repetitiously because whatsoever you do will prosper. If you meditate on the Word of God, it will help you change the image and direction of your life.

> *My son, attend to my words;*
> *incline thine ear unto my sayings.*
> *Let them not depart from thine eyes;*
> *keep them in the midst of thine heart.*
> PROVERBS 4:20–21

This is what we must do. We must get real, meditate, and speak the Word. We must apply the image of the Word to our lives on a daily basis to change our outlook on life. Do what the Word says! When you attend to the Word, you are meditating upon, gazing at, and speaking the Word. The Word is a part of you, and you are a part of the Word. Many times our lives do not change because we do not listen to the Word. The Word of God in you will paint an image in your life, and you will be able to rise up and get victory in that area of your life. Meditating in the Word is a continual process. You do not just do it until your needs get met. This is a lifestyle.

A person cannot change on their own. There must be meditation on knowledge, knowledge acted upon, visualization, verbalization, and internalization to get a change.

The change does not happen automatically. You will change when you get knowledge on the Word of God and act upon it. Meditating on the Word of God will bring a change in your life. You must hear the word by either speaking it or hearing someone else speak the word.

According to verse 21, you have to see it. This is a form of meditation—gazing at the Word. This means you are using your imagination to see what God sees in the Word and to say what God says in His Word. Keep them in the midst of thine heart; faith cometh by hearing and hearing by the word of God. He is talking about the Word. Joshua kept the promise in his heart. He kept meditating on the promises and talking about it. The Word began to become alive on the inside of him, and they went into the land that flowed with milk and honey.

What you talk about on a continuous basis is what you will see. It is also the way your life will go. If you begin to use your imagination to see what God has said in His Word, talk about it, meditate upon it, and see it happen, God says you will make your way prosperous. You must use your imagination day and night. This was a way of life for Joshua, and God expects us to use our imaginations as a way of life as well. When we apply this, we will see a change in our lives.

> *But be ye doers of the word, and not hearers only,*
> *deceiving your own selves.*
> JAMES 1:22

It is not going to happen overnight, but if you meditate on it day and night, it will happen. You cannot hear a good word and go home and do nothing about it. Nothing from nothing leaves nothing. If you go home and apply it in your life daily, it will work for you. You have to take the time to be a doer of the Word. It will not happen if you don't do it.

The results that we see in the body of Christ prove that most are not meditating on the Word of God. Progression has been slowed or stopped. Growth has been limited. Most love God and are reading the Word but are not meditating and seeing what God has said in His Word. This produces the inability to see where God wants them to be.

> **When you are a doer of the Word, you will get results.**

Testimony: I have always desired for my kids to have the opportunity to be educated. At one point in my life as they grew older, I began to see (visualize) all seven of my children going to college. I knew it would take the help of the Lord and hard work on my part in supplying the funds. I would confess it and work towards that goal. Today, all of my children had the opportunity to go to college or trade school, and some continued on to graduate school. I wanted my children to have the opportunity to go as far as they desired in school, and it happened.

We cannot sit and hope for something to happen.

Testimony: Many years ago I was faced with a decision. We made a quality decision that God is a healer and a deliverer. The Word of God rose up in our hearts, and we spoke the Word out in the midst of a difficult situation. Where did it come from? It came from the years we spent meditating on the word of God on healing—the Word was in us.

Be willing to wait for the promise. How many times have you given up on a promise? Decide to hold on to the promises God has given you. The Word has been tried already; you don't have to invent or make up anything—just meditate on the Word.

You must meditate on the Word of God and be willing to keep the Word of God before you. Begin to talk about what God is doing. We get around our friends and won't say anything about the Word of God. They talk about their filth and foolishness, and when you get in that environment, you get scared to talk about the things of God, what you believe, what you stand upon, and holy living. Yet you still want God's blessings upon your life and want to go to another level. It will not work that way. God told us what to do in order to be successful in life and make quality decisions—meditate day and night. Speak God's Word day and night so it can change your image and outlook upon life. God is a God of love—he gives.

BLUEPRINTS OF THE CHURCH

God spoke to me to add on to the church. When he spoke to me to do this, we planted a seed. We had to get a seed in the ground, which was our launching pad. So when the Lord did speak to me to get started, I drew the blueprints up, and after we had the blueprints drawn up, we went to the city to get a permit; they turned me down the first time. So then I began to meditate on what the Lord had told me. I came to the church and began to walk around the church, praying in the spirit and seeking the Lord. I continued to walk again and again around the church, praying in the spirit and asking the Lord to reveal to me what he was saying. When I got to the driveway while walking around the church, the Lord opened up a vision to me, showing me to go toward the street with the building. When he opened up my vision, he suspended my natural vision and opened up a spiritual vision to me. I saw in the spirit realm how the building was going to the street. Excitedly, I went to the architect and told him we were going to go out towards the street. The architect redrew the prints, and I went back downtown to the permits office. They approved it, and everything took off. I thank God that through meditating, speaking the Word, confessing the Word, and thanking Him for the Word that this supernaturally started to open up in my life.

Everybody wants to have success in life. Everybody wants abundance, but not everybody wants to apply the principles and use the tools God has put in place to help bring in the abundance. There are some things God has said in His Word that we must get a hold of and be a doer of the Word.

In this season in your life, you can experience more. There seems to be a blockage in many Christians' lives, but the Word will clear it up. The Word says in 2 Corinthians that Satan has blinded the minds of people, but the Word illuminates.

In John 1:4, the Word speaks of Jesus being the light of men. If anybody should be prosperous, it should be the people of the Kingdom. In Mark 9:23 Jesus said if thou can believe, all things are possible to them that believe. That one word indicates that no one has control of your breakthrough but you. We have been delivered from darkness. According to Colossians 1, there is an inheritance that we are due in the Kingdom. God intended for YOU to speak life by walking and talking in faith.

Meditate and Confess: I am in the Kingdom of God, which is the kingdom of light. Therefore there is an inheritance for me according to Colossians 1 . I can see, and my path is illuminated because I am a child of God and because I work the Word into every area of my life.

CHAPTER 3:
USING YOUR IMAGINATION
TO MEDITATE

And they said, Go to, let us build us a city and a tower,
whose top may reach unto heaven;
and let us make us a name, lest we be scattered abroad
upon the face of the whole earth.
And the LORD came down to see the city and the tower,
which the children of men builded.
And the LORD said, Behold, the people is one, and they
have all one language;
and this they begin to do: and now nothing will be
restrained from them, which they have imagined to do.
Go to, let us go down, and there confound their language,
that they may not understand one another's speech.
So the LORD scattered them abroad from thence upon
the face of all the earth: and they left off to build the city.

GENESIS 11:4–8

The word meditation goes beyond just speaking it. It also means to use your imagination. God is saying that whatever they meditate upon or see, they can have or do. This is one area where the church has become stuck. Many have thought that using their imagination was not biblical; therefore this powerful tool has sat without use within the body of Christ. They are looking at what they have instead of what the Word of God says. Your imagination is critical to your ability to carry out your desires. Not tapping into your imagination according to the Word of God and seeing yourself the way God sees you and doing what the Word of God says you can do will hinder your progress tremendously. You must be able to see! Every time God used a man mightily in the Bible, He asked him whether he could see. He was not talking about his natural eyes or the physical realm but the spiritual realm.

The eyes of your understanding being enlightened;
that ye may know what is the hope of his calling,
and what the riches of the glory of his inheritance in the saints,
And what is the exceeding greatness of his power to us-
ward who believe,
according to the working of his mighty power.
EPHESIANS 1:18–19

If you cannot see it, you cannot go there. If you cannot paint an image of what God has said in his Word, it will not manifest in your life. This will cause you to take lapses in life because you are looking at the problems and circumstances. Stop focusing on the negative things in your life and seeing yourself as a failure. Meditate on God's Word, and see yourself the way God see you. Do not allow your mind to go

> **The mind will want to take you to negative things, but you must cast down those imaginations.**

there. You may not be able to see yourself blessed and on top, but you should speak the Word of God and use it to paint pictures of what God says about you.

(For the weapons of our warfare are not carnal,but mighty through God to the pulling down of strong holds;)
Casting down imaginations,
and every high thing that exalteth itself against the knowledge of God, and bringing into captivity every thought to the obedience of Christ;

2 CORINTHIANS 10:4–5

In Genesis 11:5–6, the people had to do several things to get the blessings of God to flow into their lives. In order for them to build a tower in the natural realm, they had to get on one accord and talk about their plan. God wanted them to be blessed, but they had one thing that did not line up with the Word of God—they wanted to make a name for themselves. They talked about their plan to one another, got on one accord, and went to another level with it. If we keep the Word of God in our mouth and get it in our hearts, we can go to another level of meditation. "And now nothing will be restrained from them which they have imagined to do" (verse 6). God intends for us to use our imaginations on a daily basis to get the job done so that He can take us to the level he wants us to be. God came down and confounded their language so they could not communicate with one another, but he did not destroy their imaginations.

WHAT YOU SEE YOU CAN HAVE

And the LORD said unto Abram,
after that Lot was separated from him, Lift up now thine
eyes, and look from the place where thou art northward,
and southward, and eastward, and westward:
For all the land which thou seest, to thee will I give it,
and to thy seed forever. And I will make thy seed as the
dust of the earth: so that if a man can number the dust of
the earth, then shall thy seed also be numbered.
Arise, walk through the land in the length of it and in the
breadth of it; for I will give it unto thee.

GENESIS 13:14-17

God taught Abram the same principle. God knew that Abram had two eyes to see, but He was not talking about his natural eyes. He was not telling him to walk the land out northward, southward, eastward, and westward. He was telling him to use his imagination. God was talking about envisioning. The word "see" means to envision, use his perception, and use his imagination. He meant for Abram to use his imagination to see it in his mind in order to meditate upon it day and night. He began to talk about the stars and the sand upon the seashore. He wanted Abram to see all the land God had promised him. He was telling Abraham that whatever you can envision, see within, and meditate upon I will give to you. God also changed his name from Abram to Abraham so that every time someone would say Abraham, he would see himself as being the father of a multitude.

*By faith Abraham, when he was tried, offered up Isaac:
and he that had received the promises offered up his only
begotten son, of whom it was said,
That in Isaac shall thy seed be called: accounting that
God was able to raise him up, even from the dead;
from whence also he received him in a figure.*

HEBREWS 11:17–19

God also systematically taught Abraham the principle of meditation when he offered His only son as a sacrifice. Isaac was the promised child, but Abraham was able to see spiritually that God would raise up His son if he offered him as a sacrifice. He used his imagination to see it in his mind. Abraham used his imagination to see his son dead and God raising him up in a figure.

**We must cast down everything that is contrary
or comes against the knowledge of God.**

It must be rooted out of our subconscious minds. You must put the things of God in so that you can have a righteous conscience and make decisions based on righteousness. As long as it lines up with the Word of God, you can use your imagination for it. If your imagination takes you somewhere that doesn't line up with the Word of God, you must cast it down. If you can pull down the imagination of something wrong, you can use it to get the good things from God. God intends for us to use our imaginations. You must use your imagination to see what God sees and what God says in the Word by releasing your imagination, seeing it in the spiritual realm, and bringing it into the physical realm. When you make decisions based upon what God has said, there will be a process that you will have to go through. Satan will bring pressure to make you think it does not take all of that. He will try to get you to go back to your old mindset. Do not go there! Stick with the Word of God and the principles of God, and they will take you to another level.

We emphasize the Word of God, which we should because he tells us to keep the Word before us day and night, but in speaking God's Word, it will paint pictures in you if you use your imagination properly. You must see what God has said using your imagination. Visualize it. See it. Paint a picture with your imagination.

CHAPTER 4:
CHANGE YOUR IMAGE OF YOURSELF

But what saith it? The word is nigh thee,
even in thy mouth, and in thy heart:
that is, the word of faith, which we preach;
ROMANS 10:8

Take a look at your life. Why have you been spinning around and around, unable to get out of the situation you are in? You have been gazing and meditating on the wrong thing. Hasn't the Lord told you that your needs are met now according to His riches in glory by Christ Jesus? Why are you not reflecting upon that? We look at what we have instead of the answer. The answer is what God has said in His Word. You must focus on what God says and attract that. He said you are already blessed. Why don't you see yourself as blessed? Nothing can stop you from succeeding in life if you understand vision and meditation. The reason people are not being blessed is because they cannot see themselves as blessed. They can't imagine it. They are not gazing and meditating on the right thing. It is amazing how the Word of God says so much about blessing His people, but we see little of it in the body of Christ. This means the powerful tools of meditating and seeing themselves the way God sees them are not being used.

SPEAK IT! SEE IT!

Give, and it shall be given unto you; good measure, pressed down, and shaken together, and running over, shall men give into your bosom.
For with the same measure that ye mete withal it shall be measured to you again.

LUKE 6:38

God is telling us that the Word must first be spoken out of your mouth, and then it will be planted in your heart. This is the creative ability of God developing on the inside of you. Then you will get pictures or images of the Word of God painted on the inside of you. Many people in the body of Christ have a lot of word in them, but they are not using their imagination to see it come to pass. You can have a lot of word in you and know a lot about the Word, but your thoughts can be natural thoughts of the way the world system is set up instead of how God's system is set up. In order to go where God wants you to go and tap into the unlimited power, you must take the Word, get it in you, and use your imagination to see what God has said in His word on a continual basis. This is a lifestyle.

Your subconscious mind houses everything you have done from birth until present. This is why when you try to change, you find yourself doing the same thing you have always done. Your subconscious mind is like a computer—it will give out only what is in it. This is why God told Joshua to meditate day and night—so it would get in his subconscious mind and heart. So when the time comes to make a major decision in your life, your subconscious mind will push the Word out, and you will be able to make a quality decision.

In the body of Christ, people have habits that they are unable to break because they are not meditating on the Word of God.

Why so much lack?

One reason there are so many Christians not walking in abundance today is because they have used their imagination to see themselves as poverty stricken. They see themselves as never having enough. Their negative words have defeated them automatically. The image or picture they are looking for will not come up. Do not allow your mind to focus on poverty, debt, sickness, or failures. Use your imagination day and night to meditate on the Word.

How do you see yourself?

Whichever way you choose to see yourself, this is what you will attract. You must say what God says and see what God says in His Word.

If you're in debt, I challenge you to begin lining up your actions, meditations, and visioning with God's Word. Have you ever wondered why debt follows you or why you can't get out of that situation? That is what you have attracted as you have been meditating, pondering, speaking, and gazing upon it. God says you can have whatever you meditate upon, but according to Joshua, it must be done day and night. We can take the principle in Genesis 11:6, apply it into our lives day and night, begin to paint the image in our lives, and what we are believing for will manifest. You will attract what you continuously think about. You must bring your thoughts higher to see what God is saying in His Word and begin to gaze, mutter, and talk about it.

Can you see yourself out of debt? Can you see yourself blessed? Can you see yourself healed? Or do you see yourself defeated in life? Once again, unfortunately, here is where many Christians are today. They have plenty of word in them, but they are meditating upon what they have instead of what God says is their right to have. It's not a part of their inward spirit. Most self-made millionaires had to see themselves as a millionaire before it manifested in their lives. Stop seeing yourself as broke, and instead say what God says. It will not cost you anything to say what God says by beginning to meditate on what you believe for and visualizing it on a continual basis.

Order has already been established.

Does the grass have any problem growing? No, the earth has no problem producing, and the trees have no problem growing either. We as children of God should have no problem getting our needs met. It should come automatically if we understand the principles God has in His Word, apply them into our lives, and meditate day and night. The blessings will automatically come to you just as the earth brings forth automatically. These are principles and laws. Your mind is designed to produce what-

41

ever you are thinking about. We have awesome minds, but we must learn how to operate them based on God's plan. God says he knows the plan he has for you—a plan of peace, joy, and happiness so you can live a prosperous life.

Peace! Right Here! Right Now!

The frustration, fighting, and struggling are not from God. They are from the pit of hell and must be removed from your life. Walk in peace, let the life of God flow in you, and refuse to allow anger and frustration to come into your life. If you allow it to come, that's the way you will go. Our bodies were made to live lives of peace, not stress. When stress comes, something happens to the other parts of your body. God did not intend for us to walk in stressful conditions. He wants us to live the best life we can in the earth.

To begin feeling more confident about yourself, begin to exercise imaging yourself in the image and likeness of who God intended you to be by reading, speaking, meditating on, and envisioning it. Your subconscious mind sends a signal regarding the thing you have been saying and imagining as well as what you will feel and do. You have to see yourself the way God sees you and paint a picture according to God's Word.

And the LORD shall make thee the head, and not the tail; and thou shalt be above only, and thou shalt not be beneath; if that thou hearken unto the commandments of the LORD thy God, which I command thee this day, to observe and to do them.

DEUTERONOMY 28:13

A lot of people have problems with this scripture because they cannot see themselves being the head. You must leave the realm of the natural and meditate on the things that make you the head. At your job, you should see yourself as the head and increasing. See yourself being on time, producing more, neatly dressed, respecting your job, and being faithful.

You must learn how to use your imagination in line with what God has said; then begin to speak it out, see it, and meditate upon it. If you start talking about it and seeing yourself walking in it, then it will manifest. Stop seeing yourself as a failure. You can take your business to another level if you can see it. Nothing will be restrained from you that you have imagined. You must take your imagination and see and visualize it in light of what God's Word has promised you. It may not look like it in the natural, but you must see it in the spirit realm. Begin to say that I am the head and not the tail. It may not look like it in the natural realm, but you cannot let what you see in the natural govern your life. Do not look at the situation the way it is. Look at it through meditation, see what God sees, and feel good about yourself. Do not focus on the problem—focus on the answer.

Supernatural revelation will come when you begin to meditate and see yourself prospering.

When you receive revelation knowledge from the Word of God and apply it into your life, you will see a manifestation of the Word of God operating in your life. When you paint an image of it, as far as your mind is concerned, you have gone there even though your body did not go there with you. When your mind goes there on a continual basis, things in the spirit world will begin to supernaturally open up. Astronauts go to space based upon laws and principles. Doctors operate on people based upon laws and principles.

STAY FOCUSED!

Testimony: On one of my projects, I had a plan to finish a wall with 2,300 bricks in it. I planned the night before and pictured the wall finished during my prayer time. I used my imagination and meditated upon getting the wall completed. When I arrived at work the next morning, the bricklayers did not show up. I said, "Devil, you are a liar. The wall is finished." I got on the wall and started work. A laborer grabbed his trowel and started spreading. In one hour, 500 bricks were laid. I envisioned it before I arrived. Later on, the bricklayers arrived. They were surprised at how many bricks were laid and began to work. We all began working together. When I arrived at work, I gave the laborers the plan for the day. I told them that the wall would be finished and they could begin setting up the next wall. I used my imagination to see it completed. The wall was completed by 2:30 with only two bricklayers—2,300 bricks. I received more blessing from it than anyone else because I had meditated upon it and brought it to pass. I did not stop because something unexpected happened. I stayed focused.

Many times believers hear the Word, meditate upon the Word, and receive the Word, and then something unexpected happens. We lose our focus, our plan, our insight, our vision, and our imagination because things didn't go the way we thought they should go. We begin to think that the Word doesn't work and begin to take lapses in life. You must stay focused on what you are believing God for by meditating, using your imagination, and seeing it already done in line with the Scriptures. The Bible says you can have whatever you say.

Begin today by releasing your imagination, meditating upon the Word of God, and feeling good about yourself, and the universe (spirit realm) will give you what's yours supernaturally. You attract what you believe. It is a mindset. The battle is won or lost in the mind. We have to get our spirit, soul, and body lined up with the Word of God. Your feelings will affect your mindset; therefore you must feel good about yourself based on the Word of God. Stay focused, and do not receive any negative reports.

Receive only what God has said about you.

Let the Word of God perfect the image on the inside of you rather than the world's system or society. Always feel good about yourself.

> *For as he thinketh in his heart, so is he.*
> PROVERBS 23:7

What you think upon is what you will see, so paint pictures in your mind, write it down on paper, and do it. What have you been thinking about for the last ten or twelve years? What have you been saying the last ten or twelve years? What have you been doing during this time? Is it time for a change in your life? Is it time to start meditating on the Word of God and to start using your imagination? The time is now to allow the Word of God to paint a picture and give an image in your life so that you can see what God sees and what God says about you in His Word. Rise up and be a doer of it. You must change your way of thinking before you can change your situation. If you cannot think right, you will not be able to accomplish the things you want to do. The Word will change your way of thinking. Bringing old thought patterns into the kingdom of God won't work.

You don't have to live in poverty and lack. You live like that because you don't understand the principle of meditation. Began to receive the greater blessings of God according to the Word. One to two percent of society has all the money. There is something wrong with this picture. God promises us abundance and no lack. Get your Bible, and look in the concordance to see how many times God talks about meditation. He says if you want to be successful, meditate on the Word. The devil fights you in this area because he knows that you will see something and begin to form a new image of your life. A change will take place, and he does not want you to change or to be able to see in the spirit realm with your imagination.

We operate on a daily basis based on our level of faith. If the Word is working in you, you can operate on a higher level of faith. You will make your own way prosperous by speaking the Word of God. It will help you change your image. When you have done this, you will be able to see what God has said in His Word. Your old image will change, and God will give you a new outlook on yourself and your life.

THE "I AM" EXERCISE

Take a moment before moving forward in the book to meditate on the truth of the Word of God and what it says about you and your image. Read out loud the "I Am" statements and the scriptures as reinforcement.

I am <u>valuable</u>.

Matthew 10:29–31: What is the price of two sparrows—one copper coin? But not a single sparrow can fall to the ground without your Father knowing it. And the very hairs on your head are all numbered. So don't be afraid; you are more valuable to God than a whole flock of sparrows.

I am <u>created in the image of God</u>.

Genesis 1:27: So God created man in his own image, in the image of God created he him; male and female created he them.

I am the righteousness of God.

2 Corinthians 5:21: For he hath made him to be sin for us, who knew no sin; that we might be made the righteousness of God in him.

I am more than a conqueror in him.

Romans 8:37: Nay, in all these things we are more than conquerors through him that loved us.

I am free from the law of sin and death.

Romans 8:2: For the law of the Spirit of life in Christ Jesus hath made me free from the law of sin and death.

I am submitted to God, and the devil flees from me.

James 4:7: Submit yourselves therefore to God. Resist the devil, and he will flee from you.

CHAPTER 5:
THE POWER OF THE TONGUE

Death and life are in the power of the tongue:
and they that love it shall eat the fruit thereof.
PROVERBS 18:21

Faith cometh by hearing and hearing by the word of God. Joshua got the Word in him by speaking it. You must learn to speak the Word of God just as you did the "I am" exercise. In order to see a real change in your life, the Word must be in your mouth. This principle is called verbalization—you are speaking and talking about the Word of God day and night. The enemy does not want you to speak God's Word. He wants you to keep your mouth closed. If we keep speaking the Word of God in our mouths, it will take root in our hearts. Once it takes root in your heart, it will form an image (visualization). You will then be able to see what God has said in His Word. You are either speaking life or death into your situations and circumstances. Meditate on the right thing for the right results.

Thou art snared with the words of thy mouth,
thou art taken with the words of thy mouth.

PROVERBS 6:2

The word snared means trapped. Satan uses our words to trap us. If our words are not focused on the Word of God, they are not profitable. When we meditate on the wrong thing, we see the wrong thing. When we see the wrong thing, we do the wrong thing.

And Jesus answering saith unto them,
Have faith in God. For verily I say unto you,
That whosoever shall say unto this mountain,
Be thou removed, and be thou cast into the sea;
and shall not doubt in his heart, but shall believe that
those things which he saith shall come to pass;
he shall have whatsoever he saith.

MARK 11:22–23

Whatever you are saying is what you will receive. Having faith in God means to have the God kind of faith. Jesus is saying that if you have the wrong words in your mouth, those are the results you will get in life. Those unproductive words will produce in your life—and you will have whatsoever you said. Every mountain in our lives can be moved by speaking the Word of God.

Let the word of Christ dwell in you richly in all wisdom;
teaching and admonishing one another in psalms and
hymns and spiritual songs,
singing with grace in your hearts to the Lord.

COLOSSIANS 3:16

The Word of God must be in your mind. If you are thinking about negative things, those are the things you will begin to meditate upon and see. Many times we are speaking the Word but not meditating on the Word. We are not painting an image or envisioning what God has said in His Word into your mind.

Stop saying, "I can't. I'll never have anything. God doesn't want me blessed. I'll never own a house. I'll never have anything." The Bible says you can do all things through Christ Jesus who strengthens you. You must put the Word of God in your mouth. Start speaking it, start meditating upon it, gazing upon it, and painting a picture, and see yourself blessed. If you can see it, you can go there. When it gets in your mouth it will begin to create an image and cause you to see. Once you see it, you can bring your body along to accomplish it. You must be able to see what God says and use your imagination to see yourself as God sees you. When your corresponding actions and your emotions line up with the Word of God, this is an example of internalization. When your body lines up, you will be able to go there and see a manifestation of the Word of God in your life. The earth itself will bring it forth. You will make your way prosperous.

Do not allow laziness or the lack of understanding of the process of meditation to hinder you. Be diligent and determined concerning meditation, and be sure you are learning from leaders that encourage the practice. Meditating on the Word of God will cause the blessings to come. The wisdom of God will flow in your life.

But what saith it?
The word is nigh thee, even in thy mouth, and in thy
heart: that is, the word of faith, which we preach;
ROMANS 10:8

When you speak God's Word and hear yourself say what God is saying, faith will rise up in your heart, and the word will be deposited into your spirit.

The entrance of thy words giveth light;
it giveth understanding unto the simple.
PSALM 119:130

There are several things that happen when the Word of God is in your mouth and makes its way into your heart:

1. It brings light to you.

2. It causes a person to see. When the Bible talks about seeing, many times it is referring to seeing with your spiritual eyes.

   a. Psalm 135:16–17 – They have mouths, but they speak not; eyes have they, but they see not; they have ears, but they hear not; neither is there any breath in their mouths.

      i. Many today have eyes, but they cannot see. You can have the Word of God in you, but if you don't practice meditation, you will not understand or see it. They are not able to see in the realm of the spirit. They are not able to hear God speak to them with their spiritual ears.

3. The Word of God paints pictures in your life.

4. The Word of God planted in your heart gives you wisdom and knowledge.

5. The more light, the greater the revelation. The more Word of the Lord that you meditate upon, the more revelation you will receive from the Word of God.

6. The Word brings understanding.

God expects us to call for what we want by faith. Your tongue must become a pen of a ready writer.

Meditating in the Word is a spiritual practice. You begin by speaking the Word of God and applying it in your life. Then you go into the soulish realm and begin to visualize it. If you can't see it, you won't be able to accomplish the job you want to do. You must use your imagination to see what the Word of God declares about you. The body will bring forth actions and imaginations of what you have meditated upon.

THE "SPEAK LIFE" EXERCISE

Proverbs 18:21: Death and life are in the power of the tongue: and they that love it shall eat the fruit thereof.

According to Proverbs 18:21, life and death are in the power of the tongue. Began to incorporate your power as a believer, and take a moment to speak life over every situation that concerns you. For any situation that is challenging your faith, speak life to it today by stating and meditating on the following confession statement.

According to Proverbs 18:21, death and life are in the power of the tongue, and I boldly confess that today in the name of Jesus, I speak life to _____

_____ .

*Repeat as many times as you need, filling in the blank with various situations, and begin to exercise your speaking power and authority.

CHAPTER 6:
WE ARE MORE THAN ABLE

And the LORD spake unto Moses, saying,
send thou men, that they may search the land of Canaan,
which I give unto the children of Israel:
of every tribe of their fathers shall ye send a man,
everyone a ruler among them.

NUMBERS 13:1-2

God instructed Moses to send men to check the land out to see if it was exactly as he had said, a land flowing with milk and honey. The key point in the second verse is that God had already given them the land. It was theirs. Whenever God gives you something, he does not take it back. It belongs to you. You have to rise up in faith, receive it, and go forth to possess it by faith. This is God's way. God promised the children of Israel the land of Canaan. After Moses sent the spies out to search the land, some of them came back with an evil report.

Equipping yourself correctly will support you as you make the necessary changes you desire for a more fulfilling life. Meditating on the Word day and night will help you change your mindset from a traditional viewpoint to what God has said. So many people today are caught up in the tradition of men, they are stuck in the mud, and can't see a way out because they refuse to meditate on the Word and make changes. They refuse to use their imaginations for a righteous cause.

And they went and came to Moses, and to Aaron, and to all the congregation of the children of Israel, unto the wilderness of Paran, to Kadesh;
and brought back word unto them, and unto all the congregation, and showed them the fruit of the land. And they told him, and said, we came unto the land whither thou sentest us, and surely it floweth with milk and honey; and this is the fruit of it.
Nevertheless the people be strong that dwell in the land, and the cities are walled, and very great: and moreover we saw the children of Anak there. The Amalekites dwell in the land of the south: and the Hittites, and the Jebusites, and the Amorites, dwell in the mountains: and the Canaanites dwell by the sea, and by the coast of Jordan. And Caleb stilled the people before Moses, and said, Let us go up at once, and possess it; for we are well able to overcome it. But the men that went up with him said, we be not able to go up against the people; for they are stronger than we. And they brought up an evil report of the land which they had searched unto the children of Israel, saying, The land, through which we have gone to search it, is a

land that eateth up the inhabitants thereof; and all the people that we saw in it are men of a great stature. And there we saw the giants, the sons of Anak, which come of the giants: and we were in our own sight as grasshoppers, and so we were in their sight.

NUMBERS 13:26–33

They came back and showed them some of the fruit of the land, which meant the land was exactly as God had said. Notice their statement "surely it flows … and this is the fruit of it." The land was a land that flowed with milk and honey just as God had said. If we get a hold of the promises of God and apply them in our lives on a daily basis, our image and outlook upon life will change. Caleb rose up and said, "We are well able. Let us go up at once and possess it." He had the promise that God promised him. God had given it to him. God told Joshua to send the men out, and they checked it out. Everything lined up. No matter what is there in the land, when God has given you the land and told you it is yours, it's time to rise up and possess it.

> ## We are well able to overcome every circumstance, every hardship, and every problem!

Begin to see yourself well able. When you don't see yourself as well able, you come up with an evil report like the other spies came up with. It comes down to mindset—all the men went out and saw the same thing that Joshua and Caleb saw. They all saw the land flowing with milk and honey, but ten came back with an evil report saying we be not able. Joshua and Caleb rose up and said we are well able. God has given it to us. Let us go up and possess it.

Unbelief set in because of their tradition. They didn't believe they could have the land. They started looking at the walls, the giants, and the things in the land. When God says it's yours, it's yours—rise up and possess it with faith. You are well able to overcome it. Joshua and Caleb grabbed a hold of the promise of God that the land was theirs. Do not let anyone bring you an evil report and cause you to dwell on the negative part of life. See the answer. See what God has said, and meditate upon it so you can go forth and do the things God has called you to do.

And Caleb stilled the people before Moses, and said,
Let us go up at once, and possess it;
for we are well able to overcome it.
But the men that went up with him said,
we be not able to go up against the people;
for they are stronger than we.
NUMBERS 13:30-31

Caleb spoke among a group of unbelievers, who came with an evil report. He said we are well able. In verse 31, they came back with an evil report and said the people in the city are stronger. When God has given you a word/land, all you have to do is rise up by faith and possess it. Different mindsets and environments cause people to not see what God has said in His Word. God told Moses to send spies to check the land of Canaan out to see if it was the land flowing with milk and honey. Moses sent the spies, and the land did flow with milk and honey. It was exactly as God had said in his Word. God said I have given you the land, and the twelve spies went out.

Then the children of Judah came unto Joshua in Gilgal: and Caleb the son of Jephunneh the Kenezite said unto him, Thou knowest the thing that the LORD said unto Moses the man of God concerning me and thee in Kadeshbarnea.
Forty years old was I when Moses the servant of the LORD sent me from Kadeshbarnea to espy out the land; and I brought him word again as it was in mine heart. Nevertheless my brethren that went up with me made the heart of the people melt:
but I wholly followed the LORD my God.
And Moses sware on that day, saying, Surely the land whereon thy feet have trodden shall be thine inheritance, and thy children's forever, because thou hast wholly followed the LORD my God.
And now, behold, the LORD hath kept me alive, as he said, these forty and five years, even since the LORD spake this word unto Moses, while the children of Israel wandered in the wilderness: and now, lo, I am this day fourscore and five years old. As yet I am as strong this day as I was in the day that Moses sent me: as my strength was then, even so is my strength now, for war, both to go out, and to come in.
Now therefore give me this mountain, whereof the LORD spake in that day; for thou heardest in that day how the Anakims were there, and that the cities were great and

fenced: if so be the LORD will be with me, then I shall be able to drive them out, as the LORD said.

JOSHUA 14:6-12

This is the new generation after the old generation had died out. Joshua is in command now. Forty years have passed, and the children of Israel have not yet entered into the land God promised them. They are faced with the same scenario they had forty years ago. This group said let's take a step of faith and get what God has promised us. The other group from forty years ago said we be not able.

According to verse 7, Joshua had the Word in his heart. He meditated on **the promise of God for 40 years and kept it alive. He spoke it, gazed at it, talked about it, and saw it.** The other 10 spies died and were unable to possess the land that flowed with milk and honey. Their vision was not there—they could not see. If you can see it, you can go there. No matter what baggage is facing you, what wall is there, what problem you come against, if you can meditate, see, and gaze upon overcoming it, God can take you there. When the promise gets in your heart, you have a different image of life itself.

Joshua gave a great example of keeping the promises of God in your heart. This is a direct effect of meditation. I'm not coming down on the body of Christ. I'm trying to bring home a point here. I want you to see the difference between meditating on the Word of God and leaving the church and then not doing anything with the Word. You have to get the Word in you. This is what God told Joshua. You must keep it before you day and night to change your image from your upbringing and to change your environment. To get your mind right with God, you must meditate on the Word of God. Your decisions in life do not only affect you; they also affect your family and those around you. The promise was in Joshua, and he meditated upon it day and night; therefore Joshua and his family were able to go into the land that flowed with milk and honey.

Joshua was now 85 years old, and the promise was still alive in him because he was visualizing and meditating upon the promise. He could have forgot about the promise or could have said, "Oh well, the men brought back an evil report, and the majority wins, so we just won't make it. We will just settle for what we have," but he didn't. How many times do we settle for second best or third best instead of rising up and settling for what God has already declared in His Word? How many times have we dropped our level of faith down and said, "Oh well, it must not be meant for me. I'm just going to be happy and settle with the little bit I have and just be content with this. I'm not going to worry about it." When you think like this, you let the devil in.

This inheritance was not only for them; it was also for their children. When the spies came back with an evil report, they not only suffered but their children missed out on the greater blessings of God. Joshua kept the Word of God alive for 45 years, and then they went into the land that flowed with milk and honey. You can go where God says you can go if you keep the Word before you and meditate on it. Joshua was gazing at the land that flowed with milk and honey by meditating on the

Word of God. He saw himself in the land. Many people cannot see themselves the way God sees them, and their growth is stunted as they try to fight their way out. The way out is to meditate on the Word of God. This will cause you to see and go where God has promised you supernaturally. Joshua said he was as strong today as when God gave Moses the promise. What made him strong? He meditated on the word of God, kept the promise before him, and spoke the promise declaring what God had said in His Word. The Word was alive inside of him and made him strong.

Because God said the land belonged to Israel, Caleb also could visualize and see himself living in the land. The report was alive in his heart. **Is the report God gave you alive in your heart? Can you see it, and are you holding fast to the confession of your faith concerning it?** God's Word was alive in him. God will prosper you if you can believe it. Doors will open for you.

The promise belongs to you. As you meditate on the Word, the Word will change your image and outlook on life. It will show you God's plan for your life, and you will be able to hold fast to the promise of God. How was Joshua able to rise up after 45 years and say give me this mountain? It was in his heart. Your change also starts there. Remember, be aware of your subconscious mind and traditional thinking brought about by your environment or your upbringing—it seeks to hold you back. Go forth in God, and conquer as He intended you to do. Allow your subconscious to work for you and not against you.

CHAPTER 7:
BEWARE OF YOUR ENVIRONMENT

Be not deceived:
evil communications corrupt good manners.

1 CORINTHIANS 15:33

Your environment plays a vital role to your success in life. Who you associate with, fellowship with, and spend time with will affect your beliefs and the way you act. The wrong environment will hinder you from achieving all that God has for you. Joshua and Caleb were the only two people who stood on the promise that God had given them the land. The people who came with an evil report affected three million people. That generation had to die out until God rose up another generation with faith in His promises. The other spies were caught up in tradition, in the way they were raised, and the environment that came out of bondage in Egypt. The ten spies did not believe they could have the land.

How many times in your life have you seen yourself wanting to progress in life, but tradition, your environment, and your upbringing kept you from making a move? This is why meditating on the Word of God is vitally important. It will change your mindset and image from your upbringing and past environment.

After God brought the children of Israel out of the land of Egypt to the mountain, he gave Moses instructions to go up and possess the land. He sent ten men, and Caleb stood up and said we are well able. How many times has the door opened for you and you said I'm not able? The way you are thinking is a result of the way you were brought up—your environment. You cannot see yourself going forward and doing the things God has told you are already yours. God already told you that you can have it.

Twelve men saw the same thing, but only two held to the promise and saw the situation differently. Ten spies came back with an evil report that affected an entire generation. They wandered around in the wilderness forty years because the majority said we be not able. Your environment is vitally important. This is why God told Joshua to meditate on the Word day and night—he would change his image of his life and begin to see what God sees as he began to press forward toward the things God promised him.

Many times we allow unbelief, tradition, or our upbringing to stop us from developing and going forth in the things of God. These things are housed in your subconscious mind. You need to change your image and get the word of God in your heart and mind so you can see what God sees and do what God has said in His Word. Then you will be able to observe some things and rise up to do them. But until you begin to meditate on the Word day and night, the old pattern of your environment will keep coming up and causing setbacks. You will be good one day and set back the next day. You will be going forward one day and set back the next day. The things in your subconscious mind have to be rooted out by meditating on the Word of God day and night.

A double minded man is unstable in all his ways.
JAMES 1:8

Blessed is the man that walketh
not in the counsel of the ungodly,
nor standeth in the way of sinners,
nor sitteth in the seat of the scornful.
PSALM 1:1

A man is blessed if he does not receive counsel from the ungodly and refrains from acting like them. Your environment is critical to your life when it comes to you going forward in life. Remove yourself from the company of people with a lot of unbelief, people that are not going anywhere, people that are satisfied where they are, and people that are drinking and partying all the time and not thoughtful about the things of God—even people that are wealthy and proud individuals that feel they have accomplished their success through the power of their own hands. Especially do not date men or women that are not lined up with the Word of God.

How many times does the Word of God tell us to come out from among them? We let our tradition and environment get in the way. If you have friends that you can't counsel about righteousness and tell them what the Lord says, consider it a sign and move on. It will affect your increase in life and your progress in the things of God. You will be unable to see the direction that God is leading you in because of your friends. Speak to them, love them, but keep going on your way.

Our past environment is another area that is dangerous when it comes to the things of God and going to another level. The world's system has done a job on the minds of people. Decide to reach up, grab the promises by faith, and meditate upon them day and night so you do not lose hope regarding the things of God. When it comes to the things of God, we lose hope because we don't know how to take hold and meditate.

Now the LORD had said unto Abram,
Get thee out of thy country, and from thy kindred, and
from thy father's house,
unto a land that I will show thee.

GENESIS 12:1

Abraham had to change his environment. He had previously been in a pagan country where nobody was serving God. God had to call him from there so he could get Abraham's attention and minister to him. We must get into and remain in an environment where God's Word is working on a daily basis.

Wherefore come out from among them, and be ye
separate, saith the Lord, and touch not the unclean
thing; and I will receive you.

2 CORINTHIANS 6:17

This is critical to your advancement in life. God told us to meditate on the Word day and night so we can get the right image. The wrong environment will affect your growth in life and stop you from getting involved in the things of God.

> **In order to change your image, you must change your environment.**

In Numbers 13, Joshua and Caleb were the only two to stand up and say we are well able. The other ten spies brought an evil report and caused millions of people to not enter into the land that flowed with milk and honey even though God had given it to them. Choose your environment and the people you fellowship with. You can't fellowship with everybody. It will affect the way you believe God, your church attendance, and your walk in life. Many people do not believe this, but it does affect your walk and your lifestyle.

Parents, do not let your children run with just anybody. Check the people out thoroughly before you let your kids go with them. Do not agree to their requests just to please yourself so you can have some free time. It will damage your kids' lives. Don't remain around people just because you were raised with them if they are going in an opposite direction. Get out of that environment. Don't put up with it. It will damage your life and your future. Evil communications corrupt good manners. **The environment you foster dictates your future!**

In the Wrong Environment

And he said, A certain man had two sons:
And the younger of them said to his father, Father, give
me the portion of goods that falleth to me.
And he divided unto them his living.
And not many days after the younger son gathered all
together, and took his journey into a far country, and
there wasted his substance with riotous living.
And when he had spent all, there arose a mighty famine
in that land; and he began to be in want.
And he went and joined himself to a citizen of that
country; and he sent him into his fields to feed swine.
And he would fain have filled his belly with the husks
that the swine did eat: and no man gave unto him.
And when he came to himself, he said,
How many hired servants of my father's have bread
enough and to spare, and I perish with hunger!
I will arise and go to my father, and will say unto him,
Father, I have sinned against heaven, and before thee,
And am no more worthy to be called thy son: make me
as one of thy hired servants. And he arose, and came to
his father. But when he was yet a great way off, his father
saw him, and had compassion, and ran,
and fell on his neck, and kissed him.

LUKE 15:11–20

The first thing the younger son did was change his environment, and in this new environment, he wasted his substance with riotous living. There arose a famine in the land, and he began to be in need. In the wrong environment, he was sent

69

to the field to feed swine for a Gentile farmer who raised pigs. He begin to live with the pigs and filled his stomach with the leftover food the pigs were served. In verse 17, he started to use his imagination, which is a type of meditation, about how his former life was at home. He had to change his mindset before he could change his environment. He began to speak the word. Meditate means to mutter, ponder, speak, murmur, gaze, and imagine. At his low point, his thinking began to change. In verse 18, he realized he was in the pigs' environment but was not of the pigs' kind. Change began first in his mind; then his body followed in the direction of his mindset.

> *This book of the law shall not depart out of thy mouth;*
> *but thou shalt meditate therein day and night,*
> *that thou mayest observe to do according to all that*
> *is written therein: for then thou shalt make thy way*
> *prosperous, and then thou shalt have good success.*
> JOSHUA 1:8

He made his way prosperous by speaking, muttering, and pondering to himself.

> *Thou hast caused men to ride over our heads;*
> *we went through fire and through water: but thou*
> *broughtest us out into a wealthy place.*
> PSALM 66:12

He came to his wealthy place. In verse 24, the father said, "My son was dead and is now alive again." His mindset had changed.

> *For as he thinketh in his heart, so is he:*
> PROVERBS 23:7(A)

CHAPTER 8:
RENEW YOUR MIND

And the very God of peace sanctify you wholly;
and I pray God your whole spirit and soul and body be
preserved blameless
unto the coming of the Lord Jesus Christ.
1 THESSALONIANS 5:23

Joshua had to deal with the spirit, soul, and body. Verbalization, the Word in his mouth, dealt with his spirit man. Visualization, being able to see, dealt with his soul (mindset). Your soulish realm (mind, will, intellect, imagination and emotions) has to be dealt with by God. These are the areas we have to deal with; however, this is one area saints do not do anything about, and it causes them to make the wrong decisions in life. It is because the wrong thing is housed in their subconscious mind.

Improper thinking will cripple your decision making.

It will limit your faith and prevent you from overcoming the challenges of life. We change this by maintaining a renewed mind and meditating on the Word of God on a consistent basis.

There are challenges you will face in life every day. If you have incorrect thinking that is not lined up with the Word of God, you will make the wrong decision and take lapses in life. For example, it usually takes four years to graduate from college, but when you make wrong decisions and do not stay focused, you will graduate in 10 years instead of your original plans.

In the same way, if their mind is not lined up with the Word of God, the first thing people do when it comes time to make a decision is to make decisions based upon the flesh and what they see in the natural realm. They don't base their decisions upon what God has said because they have not been meditating in the Word. Every time you are challenged with a decision in life, you must first make the decision based upon the Word of God. If your mind has not been renewed or you have not been meditating, you will make the decision based upon the natural realm. When you make a decision based upon the natural realm, it will cause you to back up from the Word of God and what you have set out to do for the kingdom of God. In order to go to another level, you must think on another level by putting the Word of God in your subconscious mind.

Thousands of thoughts come to our minds on a daily basis. We must be able to take the thoughts that comes to us that are lined up with God's Word and make our decisions based upon what God's Word says. If we don't renew our minds and meditate day and night on God's Word, we will make the wrong decision.

Beloved,
I wish above all things that thou mayest prosper
and be in health, even as thy soul prospers.
3 JOHN 2

We must deal with the spirit, body, and soul. God wants your spirit, your soul, and your body to prosper. Your soulish realm will prosper through meditation and using your imagination. You must be able to see what God says about you, meditate upon it, and let your body come into line with that. The subconscious and conscious mind speaks a unique language. They communicate in these three dimensions: (1) words – The right words will trigger things in your mind; (2) imagination – The conscious deals with imagination (soulish realm). It paints pictures for you. You must paint pictures using the Word of God; (3) feelings and emotions – Have you ever told yourself that you don't feel like doing something? Your mind receives that word, and the word sends a trigger to your body that you don't feel like doing it. It sends a signal throughout your body telling it how to feel. You begin to paint a picture in your mind. Your words and emotions affect how you feel. This is the language of the subconscious and conscious mind.

We want prosperity and to be blessed, but there is a process and some conditions we must meet. **Your potential for doing well in life is based upon your development of your mind, will, imagination, and emotions.** We must develop these areas if we expect to go to another level. These three areas are critical for the believer, and if you develop yourself in these areas, your success is limitless. There is nothing wrong with using your imagination for the Word of God. If you cannot see it within, it will not manifest in your life.

Success in life involves accurate thinking and proper management of the thought life. Why do you keep doing the same thing you have been doing for twenty years? Why are you having the same temper tantrums you had as a teenager? Why are you acting the same way? It's because the old way is dominating your subconscious mind. You have not renewed your mind and meditated on the Word on a consistent basis to root the junk out.

This process is similar to a computer. The things you put in the computer are the only things you can get out of the computer when you have a need. If you don't put the right thing in your subconscious mind, you will make a decision based upon your environment and the natural realm. God has told us to maintain a renewed mind and meditate so we can change our way of thinking and make quality decisions in life. Your confession of the Word of God is done to help you change your way of thinking so that you can think like God. According to Isaiah 55, God's thoughts are higher than our thoughts, and His ways higher than our ways. God is, in essence, telling us to change our way of thinking through meditation. You can do it because the Bible says you can. Whatever the Word says you can do, you can do. Don't allow limited viewpoints to keep you from moving forward. If you can see it and meditate upon it, you can have it.

You will attract whatever you meditate upon.

It is a supernatural act of God that will bring the manifestation into your life. We are wired this way. God has made us this way. The world's system knows exactly how we are wired. You can use the television as an example. When you watch a football game, commercials are shown over and over again. They want you to get the image in your subconscious mind so that when you go to the store, your subconscious mind will bring up that image, and you will purchase it. We must take the same concept—speak God's Word over and over, and begin to gaze and use our imaginations to see it manifesting in our lives. You must see yourself as God has said in His word.

In Numbers, we found out that God had given Joshua the land that flowed with milk and honey. Only two people entered in from their generation: Joshua and Caleb. The old generation had a negative and unbelieving mindset. God had to allow the older generation to die out because of their negative attitude. Joshua and Caleb were the only two during that generation to have a positive mindset. They saw what God said and said let us go up and possess it because we are well able.

Whatever God has promised you in His word is yours. Practice meditation to get it in your subconscious mind so you will be able to walk it out. After 40 years had expired, Joshua and Caleb still had the promise alive in their hearts and minds. Joshua and Caleb rose up and said give me this mountain. Joshua's mindset was in the Promised Land. He talked about it, visualized it, and meditated upon it, and he and his family went in. No matter what you are going through or facing in life, the key to success is meditating in the Word. You must see what God has said, activate your faith, and hold fast to the Word in the midst of chaos. Don't back up from the Word, coming to church, and the things of God. You cannot run when the devil brings negativity. In difficult times, you must stand on the Word. You are where you are today because of your decision making.

Now unto him that is able to do exceeding abundantly
above all that we ask or think,
according to the power that worketh in us.
EPHESIANS 3:20

Whatever you ask God for, think about, see, envision, meditate upon, and imagine that God is able to do that and more. You can have it as long as you live a consistent Christian lifestyle. He said you can profit from these things.

Finally, brethren, whatsoever things are true,
whatsoever things are honest,
whatsoever things are just,
whatsoever things are pure,
whatsoever things are lovely,
whatsoever things are of good report;
if there be any virtue, and if there be any praise,
think on these things.
PHILIPPIANS 4:8

To think has the connotation to see or to use your imagination. You must think on righteous things and those things that are in line with God. He tells us what to think upon. He is telling us to change our way of thinking. Every challenge in life can be overcome by thinking right and making quality decisions. If a person does not have the Word in them, they will most likely make the wrong decision when the challenges of life come. Why won't people come to church? Why won't people give their tithes? They are not thinking in line with God's Word and meditating upon what he has promised them. The flesh will say I'm not giving my money. I'm not doing this or that. It's because they are not saturating their mind with the Word of God. We must learn this principle of meditation. To change your situation, you must change your way of thinking. These are biblical principles we must apply in our lives on a daily basis.

(For the weapons of our warfare are not carnal, but mighty through God to the pulling down of strong holds;) Casting down imaginations, and every high thing that exalteth itself against the knowledge of God, and bringing into captivity every thought to the obedience of Christ.

2 CORINTHIANS 10:4–5

DEALING WITH STRONGHOLDS

Strongholds are mental thought patterns and are hindrances to the child of God. They will keep you locked into negative beliefs, defeat, and negative behavior. It will hurt you and stop you from going forward if you do not know how to pull them down by meditating on the Word of God on a consistent basis. A stronghold may result from your upbringing, your environment, or what you have seen. If you do not root it out with the Word of God, you will find yourself making the same bad decisions that your parents and siblings made. You must get the Word and as Joshua said—meditate day and night. You make your decisions based upon what you have seen and what you know.

PARTICIPATE TO BRING YOUR PROMISE TO PASS

What is stopping you from going forward in life and believing God for all He has ordained for you? It will not happen without your participation. It will not happen just because you are a Christian. God has told us over and over again to do something with our mind. Yes, you are born again, and yes, you love God, but what about the mind? You must get out of the flesh, grab ahold of what God has said in His word, and start meditating, visualizing, seeing what he has said, and walking in the light of it. God has planned for us to live a prosperous life, but we won't get it if we are murmuring, complaining, mad, throwing temper tantrums, and angry. We will only get it from meditating on God's word day and night.

We must uproot negative core beliefs that will limit and hinder us from walking in the greater blessings of God by meditating on the Word of God. Change comes by meditating on God's Word; this is not wishful thinking. This is actually putting substance in your subconscious mind. Many today are blind and cannot see where they are going. Visualization is not working for them even though they are born again. Jesus paid the price for us and showed us how to be loosed from the enemy—meditate on God's Word.

While we look not at the things which are seen,
but at the things which are not seen:
for the things which are seen are temporal;
but the things which are not seen are eternal.

2 CORINTHIANS 4:18

God requires that we see the unseen things by using our imaginations and meditating on His Word on a daily basis. You are to envision, apply the Word in our lives, and speak the Word over and over until it gets in your subconscious mind. Then you will be able to make quality decisions in life. Make the mind receive the things of God by shifting your mind. The things which are seen are temporary and subject to pass away. If you are believing God for a new car, you should not be focusing on the car that is causing you trouble. You need to pray the prayer of faith and use your imagination to see the new car that you want. God says you can have whatever you ask or think according to the power that works in you. You must see yourself driving it, and you must speak God's Word over it. Supernaturally, you will attract that, and it will happen.

David made a decision to fight Goliath. God did not tell him to go fight him. Goliath was coming against the knowledge of God, so David made a quality decision to take the giant out. When you make a quality decision to say what God says and do what God has said to do in His Word, you trigger the supernatural ability of God. When you make a decision to be on time for church, pay your tithes, and do what is right in the sight of God, the supernatural power of God gets involved. The kingdom of God works in line with His Word. You say God's

Word, you speak God's Word, and then you see or envision God's Word working for you. If you cannot see it, it will not become a reality in your life. If you do not use your imagination, you will not be able to see the things God has said are for you. The things you cannot see in the natural realm that are based upon God's Word are in the spirit realm.

For by him were all things created, that are in heaven,
and that are in earth, visible and invisible,
whether they be thrones, or dominions,
or principalities, or powers:
all things were created by him, and for him:
COLOSSIANS 1:16

Every natural thing that is needed in life is already in existence. It is in the invisible realm. The Word of God goes into the invisible realm and brings it into the natural realm.

Something has to be working on the inside of you—the Word. To think means to use your imagination—what you see or envision. What you think about is what you will see, and what you see is what you will act upon. If you are not seeing right, you are not thinking right; if you are not thinking right, you are not making quality decisions in life. You must get your thinking right and in line with the Word of God. If you think on the right thing long enough, it will get into your subconscious mind, and you will be able to see the right thing and make the right decision. You will not have to wonder what to do or how to do it. Your subconscious mind will automatically push out what you have put in it.

Education is a good thing. We need it and have to have it, but sometimes it gets in the way. When it comes to the things of God, we should base our decisions upon what God has said in his Word.

IT'S TIME FOR KINGDOM ADVANCEMENT

Many people are stuck in the same place they were in when they came into the family of God. This is why this message is vitally important. There must be some changes that take place in your life. If there are no changes, what are you thinking about or seeing? **What is your thought life?** How are you acting in life? The Word of God must be in your mouth (verbalization). The Word of God must be meditated upon (imagination/visualization/envision). The Word of God must take root in your heart (internalization). If not, you will become satisfied with that nickel and dime job and will not go anywhere. You will sit there and rot in poverty if you don't get the promises of prosperity in your heart. You will wait for retirement only to find out it's not what you thought it was going to be. It's not enough—now look at the years you have wasted. You could have been meditating in God's Word, allowing God to give you a witty invention or other things you could use your God-given talent to do. There is more than just one thing you can do. Don't sit there and waste your life. God has put it in His word, and you have to pull it out through meditating on God's Word.

CONCLUSION

You have to begin to take the promises of God, put it in your mouth, and start speaking it. Day and night, begin to talk about the promises. Close your eyes and see yourself doing exactly what the promise has said. For example, if the Bible says he was wounded for our transgressions, bruised for our iniquities, the chastisement of our peace was upon him, and by his stripes ye are healed, you are to take that promise, speak the promise day and night every day of your life, and use your imagination to see yourself whole and delivered. When the promise consumes you, you will see a manifestation take place. It's the same way for prosperity. God promised you abundance and no lack. People cannot see themselves walking in abundance, because they are not meditating on the Word of God day and night. You must take the scriptures like **2 Corinthians 9:7–8, which says, "Every man according as he purposeth in his heart, so let him give; not grudgingly, or of necessity: for**

God loveth a cheerful giver. And God is able to make all grace abound toward you; that ye, always having all sufficiency in all things, may abound to every good work." You must continue to speak it, begin to gaze at it, and see yourself according to what God has said in His Word. When the promise consumes you and gets in your subconscious mind, you will begin to think differently and have a different outlook on life, and faith will begin to rise up on the inside of you.

It is important to get the Word into your subconscious mind so that it will come out during the time of need so you will be able to make quality decisions in life and get the best God has for you.

Joshua visualized for 40 years and saw himself in the land that flowed with milk and honey, and he went in. The other ten spies did not go in because they didn't meditate on the promise. They died out in the wilderness. The other people could have gone in if they would have ignored the negative report of the ten spies and held fast to the promise of God. Stop settling for second best. Be willing to wait on God and see His hand move in your life. Are you like the ten spies going by what they see, or are you like the two who brought back a report that we believe God is well able? In this life, we believe God or we believe the devil. Which are you?

Are you ready to go where God wants to take you? There must be some changes that only come through meditating on the Word of God. It will change your subconscious mind and change your outlook upon life. You can have ten jobs and make a lot of money, but if you do not do something about the inward part, the conscious and subconscious, and put the Word of God in you, you can be a millionaire and act the same way you acted before you came into the family of God. You must put the right thing into your subconscious mind so the right thing can come out.

Prayer for Salvation

Heavenly Father,

You said in Your Word that whosoever shall call upon the name of the Lord shall be saved, so I am calling on Jesus right now. Lord, I confess and acknowledge You with my mouth that Jesus is Lord, and in my heart, I believe and trust that You raised Him from the dead. I accept You and confess You as my Lord and Savior. Thank You, Father, for forgiving me, adopting me as Your child, and making me a new creature altogether in Christ Jesus. Amen.

If you have prayed this prayer to receive Jesus Christ as your Lord and Savior for the first time, please feel free to contact us by e-mail for prayer at believersfaithfellowship@yahoo.com or write to us at:

Believers Faith Fellowship Church
Dr. E.L. Womack, Sr.
3965 East Brookstown Drive
Baton Rouge, LA 70805
www.bffministries.org

About Dr. E.L. Womack, Sr.

Dr. E.L. Womack, Sr., was born and raised in Mobile, Alabama. He was drafted into the United States Army after high school and became a sergeant within fourteen months of entering the military. As a result of his combat in the Vietnam War, he earned a Purple Heart and many other metals. He is currently an entrepreneur and enjoys real estate investments.

After knowing his wife for only three months, on September 18, 1970, Dr. Womack and Audrey Womack were joined in unity. They are the proud parents of seven children. Now, 45 years later, the Lord continually strengthens them as they submit to each other.

In 1981 Dr. Womack attended Rhema Word of Faith School in Baton Rouge. He was licensed in 1982 and ordained in 1983 by the National Baptist Association under the late Reverend John D. Lands of Gloryland Baptist Church in Baton Rouge, Louisiana. Dr. Womack, who is a certified Christian Counselor, was honored with a doctorate of divinity from E.L. White Seminary School in Mobile, Alabama. He is also the founder of God Comfort Ministerial Alliance, Inc.

Early in his ministry, God deeply impressed Dr. Womack to teach the body of Christ "how to walk by faith." He started a Bible study in his home, and this humble beginning became

Believers Faith Fellowship Church in 1985. His ministry has impacted the lives of many ministers and pastors in the city of Baton Rouge.

Dr. Womack is a member of the Association of Independent Ministries under the direction of Drs. I.V. and Bridget Hilliard of Houston, Texas. He is also an active member of MOVE under the leadership of Dr. Adam Richardson, Sr.

He believes in the operation of the nine gifts of the Holy Spirit and teaching the uncompromised Word of God.